WALK
STICKS

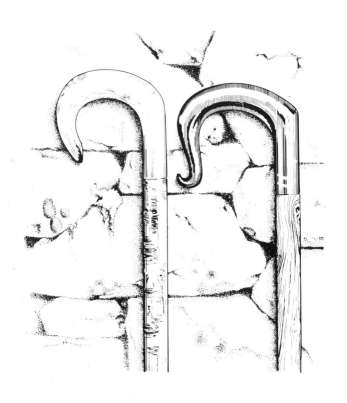

WALKING STICKS

EDWARD HART

The Crowood Press

First published in 1986 by
The Crowood Press Ltd
Ramsbury, Marlborough
Wiltshire SN8 2HR

Paperback edition 1993

This impression 1994

British Library Cataloguing-in-Publication Data

A catalogue record for this book
is available from the British Library

ISBN 1 85223 756 2

Acknowledgements
Line illustrations by Annette Findlay, from
sketches by Audrey Hart

Special thanks to the late Len Parkin for his
enthusiasm and invaluable help
(Sadly, Len Parkin died after the first edition was
published, but his family carries on his horn shop
at Hermitage, Hawick, Roxburghshire.)

Thanks also to D. R. and E. M. Lye for their assistance.

Typeset by Alacrity Phototypesetters
Banwell Castle, Weston super-Mare

Printed in Great Britain by
BPCC Hazell Books Ltd
Member of BPCC Ltd

Contents

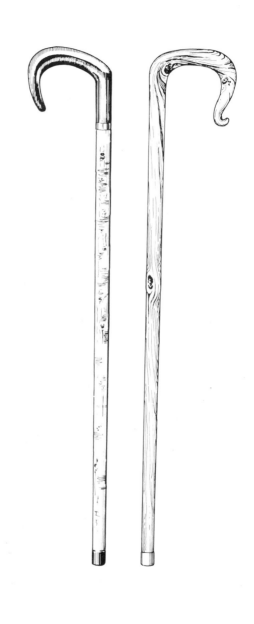

Introduction

The use of a stick is almost as old as man; it is a natural aid for walking, hunting or fighting. Sticks also represent native arts in primeval form, using the most suitable materials to hand. Ancient tombs have yielded many intricately carved sticks, and travellers to most parts of the world have returned home with collections. Sir Winston Churchill was one public figure who listed stick collecting among his hobbies, and his sticks may still be seen at Chartwell. Sticks become so much part of life that some of the keenest dressers or collectors would hardly think to list them as interests.

Canes were fashionable in Britain earlier this century; my father sported an ebony stick with a silver knob. The type I shall deal with here is fashioned from native British wood, readily available in the countryside, though horns from which to fashion the head are now scarce.

A number of different types of walking stick are to be found at the many excellent country fairs and agricultural shows. The cheaper ones are steam-bent and do not last well, but they do give an indication of the possibilities, and are an easy introduction to the stick world.

A peculiarly British branch of the art is the shepherd's crook, with horn head and wood shank, often hazel. Parts of France grow magnificent hazels in abundance, and yet not a decent stick is seen. The farmers simply cut off a green hazel and use that. Compared to a carefully dried, artistically carved stick, the green shank is clumsy. I brought back a bundle of lovely, straight, mottled French hazels after a visit, thinking that here was a year's supply of shanks. However, I was foolish enough to mention the hoard in a farming column, after which every other Dales shepherd that I met asked for one, and my supply almost vanished!

The hotbed of stick dressing in Britain is Northumberland and the Borders. Here, evening classes are staged and every local show has stick classes, where a marvellous variety of work is presented, and where competition is intensely keen. The would-be maker or collector should endeavour to visit these shows. The reason that this region leads the craft lies in the size of its farms during the late nineteenth century and early twentieth century. They were large and employed specialist shepherds, whereas over much of the rest of Britain, the farmer and his family did the shepherding. The shepherd had no further calls on his time after dark in winter; he lived in an isolated cottage with no road and no means of transport other than his own feet. This, of course, was long before television or even radio. The only light was from an oil wick, unsatisfactory for long spells of reading but adequate for stick carving, with the bonus of a ready supply of heat for softening the horn.

The true hill-man, shepherd or gamekeeper,

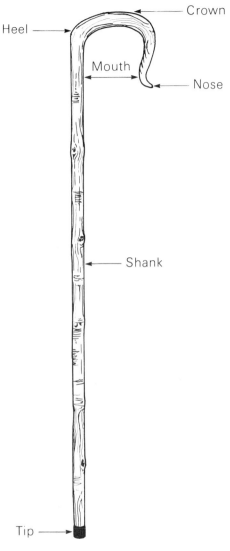

Crown

Heel

Mouth

Nose

Shank

Tip

Main parts of a walking stick or crook.

[9]

seldom leaves his abode without a stick. It is his 'third leg', helping him to make those long, loping strides essential where many miles are walked daily, and also enabling him to probe bogs and wet crossings for a safe footing. It is a source of constant amazement to me how keen city people will set off over our highest hills, without a stick amongst them. The professional hill dweller would never think of setting off without his stick.

1 · Materials

A wide range of materials can be used in stick dressing, including such unusual types as rhododendron, or even Brussels sprouts. The novice would do better to use such well-tried favourites as hazel, holly, ash and blackthorn. These are found in most lowland areas of rural Britain and in much of the uplands, although the planting of spruce over thousands of acres by the Forestry Commission and private companies has reduced the variety.

Although these suitable woods are available, they are invariably on private land. Therefore, the first step is to obtain permission from the owner, readily given in most cases to a genuine stick dresser. Stick dressing is an almost wholly beneficial occupation, and must not be spoilt by trespass and theft. If I cut a number of shanks from one source, I try to repay by making a stick for the owner.

SUITABLE TREES

Hazel
Several varieties occur, with varying degrees of mottling; an artistically mottled hazel is a thing of beauty. Remember that however intricate any final carving may be, a well-balanced, cylindrical shank is

a first essential – a good head will be spoilt by a poor shank.

Hazel is little used commercially now. It was once fashioned into hurdles and barrel hoops, and made into stack prods to keep thatch in place, but is now mainly found growing wild along streams or fringing a clearance. In southern England it was grown as a coppice crop, and coppiced every seven to ten years. Such coppices are an obvious target for the stick dresser, never forgetting the necessary permission.

Holly

A hardy tree growing on a wide range of soils, holly takes a high polish and is suitable for carving. Straight suckers may grow from the base, but these are often damaged by stock. Further straight growths sometimes occur higher up, especially if the tree has been pollarded.

Variegated hollies are planted in gardens, but bark colour is of little importance as the stems are usually peeled. Holly shanks require longer to dry than most, and Northumbrian stick dresser Norman Tulip has made some of his finest examples from holly stored for seven years.

Ash

Richard Jefferies strode his woodlands with 'a ground ash'. That is an ash sapling, with a below-ground swelling of the root which becomes the head of the stick. Such 'one-piece' sticks are very strong, and straight ones are not too difficult to find. The forester's agreement is more important than ever when selecting a ground ash, for an entire potential tree is being taken. In an ash wood they may be plentiful enough, and taken without damage to the whole.

Coppice ash is used for mass-produced walking sticks and crooks. It is easily worked when steamed, and the head bent into shape. Leave such a stick overnight in the rain and it reverts towards its original shape. This coppice wood, or growth from suckers, is not suitable for the best sticks, and has often grown too fast to be strong.

Blackthorn

The *Standard Cyclopedia of Modern Agriculture* of circa 1900 says blackthorn 'is usually frequently found among the underwood in copses, where it is an unwelcome and rather useless intruder, although its shoots make good walking sticks'.

They do. Blackthorn grows straight, with projecting spines which must be trimmed with care when shaping starts. On deep soils it grows strong and true, and spreads away from the hedge, so that removing it is beneficial. The blackthorn or sloe has snowy white flowers which appear before the leaves and are pretty in spring, and the glossy, bitter fruit is used for home-made wines. The Irish shillelagh or cudgel is usually of blackthorn.

I have found excellent blackthorns in Northamptonshire spreading from a wood. They need care in digging out, and grow so close the roots intermingle, causing some wastage when dressed,

[13]

but where they grow plentifully a store of them is a stick dresser's bonus.

Elm and Beech

Mature timber from these is used for heads. The hard knot or burr growing from the trunks is unbeatable for the purpose, and should be sought from timber yards, where it has few other uses.

Willow

There are many attractive varieties of willow, but in general the wood is not long lasting.

HORN

The pinnacle of the stick dresser's art is the horn head. That need not deter others who prefer to work solely in wood, but horn does lend itself to a wide variety of shapes and types.

Ram's Horn

This is the most popular. It comes best from a sheep of at least three years old, and after that the older the better, provided the horn is sound. As a sheep ages, it may figure in more and more fights with other males, or the horn may grow inwards to the face and need sawing off. Horns from a naturally grown hill ram are best; Jacob is now quite widespread, but its horn tends to be shelly, that is, too thin. Only the hard outer casing of a horn is of any value to the stick dresser. The inside part, containing blood vessels and nerves while the sheep was alive, can not be used.

[14]

A ram's horn before straightening and clamping.

Most lowland breeds are hornless, hence more horns are found in upland regions. These tend to be stick dressing areas, and demand far exceeds supply. Unless a ram dies naturally on the farm, his horn will not be left behind but will accompany him to the abattoir, where staff are fully aware of the value of horn, and only price and perseverence will yield a supply. No figure can be given as a guide to the value of horn, as the price has risen so quickly. Acquisition is also a constant limiting factor, as horn has many craft uses.

Ewe Horn

A nicely curved Blackface ewe horn can make a nice stick head, or a half head. Ewe horns vary in size and shape and, although easier to come by, are too slight for much decoration and too insubstantial to make a full-scale crook.

Deer Horn

This is now sold on a regular basis, but is also becoming dearer. It is suitable for walking stick heads, and first-class for thumb sticks. Look out for deformed ones; I saw one recently that became an intriguing head. Scotland and the Isles are the main sources.

Buffalo Horn

Commercially available, buffalo horn has an attractive black and also a coloured finish, and has become more popular in recent years, largely because it is often easier to obtain than ram's horn.

Cow Horn

Cow horn is difficult to shape; it is brittle and liable to snap even under heat. Nor are there many cow horns around in these days of dehorning. The nicest cow horn heads I have seen were from an Ayrshire, made by an acknowledged expert. They are for the experienced dresser who does not like to be defeated by any material, rather than for the novice.

Other horns crop up from time to time. A light,

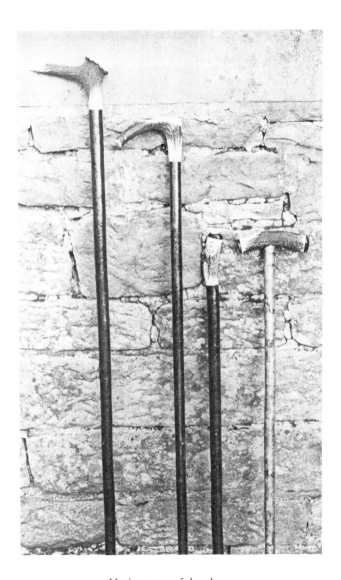

Various uses of deer horn.

[17]

Buffalo horn in unbended state, and the type of head that may be fashioned from it.

shelly case holds little hope; a solid section is needed to make a top-class head.

2 · Tools

The simplest of tools suffice to make a walking stick, but most stick dressers take a practical view and speed their work with modern gadgets. Yet we should always keep in mind the Border shepherd in his lonely cottage, whittling away with a penknife, a saw, a lamp and little else.

COLLECTING SHANKS

Spade, saw and axe are the main tools necessary when seeking shanks. A Bushman saw is light to carry and probably the best, though not so easy to use among a lot of suckers at ground level. A sharp hand saw has advantages there, but it depends on the number of people in the expedition. There is no point in being so overburdened with tools that no room is left for the sticks.

A medium axe of about 4 lb is handy and will be needed for roots. These are bared by a spade, preferably a light spade with a narrow spit, such as is used for rabbiting. Baler twine or light rope should be used to secure the bundle of shanks neatly, making them far easier to carry than a loose mass shooting out at all angles and catching in the branches of trees.

WORKSHOP TOOLS

Two great aids in the workshop are a bench and a vice. Any strong bench will serve, but a vice needs to be chosen with care. A wooden vice set flush with the side of the bench is useful for straightening shanks, and for keeping the shank secure while it is being dressed. For working the horn, a sound metal vice is essential. Shepherds who possessed no metal vice would take a consignment of horns to the local smithy, and heat and rough-shape them there. Modern variations of this method should be sought where a really strong vice is not available at home. A selection of pipe sections, wedges and levers are essential accessories at this stage.

Saws

A comprehensive range of tools adds pleasure to any job. A rip saw for cutting with the grain and a cross-cut for sawing at right angles to it are a useful start to any tool collection, and can also be used for other house and garden jobs. A Bushman has been mentioned for stick collecting expeditions, but is too inaccurate for workshop use.

Of the various types of frame saws, a bow saw is strong enough to cut out the wooden head as accurately as possible so that a minimum of rasping is needed. A fret saw is useful for fine corners and such places as the curl on the nose of a wooden head, while a coping saw is intermediate.

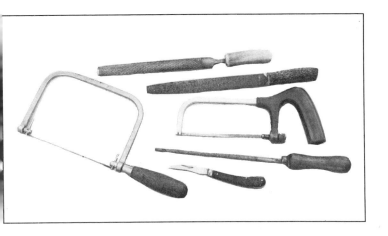

Saws, files and knives are the main tools for the job.

Files

A wide range of files is comparatively inexpensive, and will both speed the work and make it more effective. Surform files have flat, bevelled or cylindrical faces, and all on a standard frame. They are very useful in the initial stages of shaping, when large quantities of wood or horn have to be filed away. Rasps fulfil a similar function.

Other files can be bought in different sizes and different grades, from coarse to fine. If decorations are contemplated, then small, fine files reaching all the corners are essential. A wooden handle to the file makes it easier to use, and less likely to be damaged by moisture from the hand.

Knives

A really good pocket knife, kept very sharp, remains the stick dresser's chief ally. Besides its use in shaping a wooden head, it is unbeatable for removing rough horn during the heating process.

Drills

If you have an electric drill, use it. We are not concerned with using the original methods, but with continuing an old skill in a modern setting. A horn head is shanked by drilling a hole of $\frac{1}{2}$ or $\frac{5}{8}$ inch diameter into it, to take the dowel or pin on the shank. The same applies to a separate wood head.

The drill is also used to take out the underpart of a wooden head, usually more quickly than sawing round the curve.

FINISHING MATERIALS

Sandpaper and emery paper in varying grades are needed. It is essential to have a wide range of grades; to use too coarse a sandpaper on a mottled hazel shank can speedily ruin it. Similarly, too fine a paper makes little impression on file marks left on the head, which must be removed before the final polishing can begin. Steel wool and cloths complete the range.

Plastic wood is needed to fill cracks, or to hide and strengthen faults in the wood.

Polish and Varnish

Though there are a few 'secret' recipes around, polyurethane is the best cover for shanks. The clear type from any do-it-yourself shop is all that is necessary. It is amazing how even quite an ordinary stick is improved by two coats of polyurethane. Preparations like Shellac, which require mixing before use, show no advantage over polyurethane. A word of caution: do not buy a bigger tin than you are likely to use in a few weeks or months, as it hardens even if well sealed and becomes useless.

Paint

In competitive classes, paint is not allowed, except in the decorated section. Very small quantities of top-quality paints are needed here.

HORN FINISH

A horn finish is obtained simply through sand-papering and polishing, and can be aided by kitchen cleaners such as Vim. For one's own use, there is no need to seek the show table standard, yet once the stick dressing bug bites, the search for perfection intensifies, and the very smooth finish is sought.

Heat

We have seen how the early shepherds used the heat from their oil lamps to soften the horn and make it workable. A metal chimney concentrates the heat admirably. A dish of methylated spirits or an Aladdin stove give the required intensity of heat. A bottle gas burner can be used, but must be adjusted carefully or scorching will occur.

Kitchen foil wrapped round the shank during the heating process is one recommended way of protecting the bark, and damping with a wet cloth can also help.

3 · Gathering the Shanks

SEASON

Everything to do with stick making should be fun. This includes that essential preliminary, the securing of sufficient shanks for the winter's work. Stick making tends to be a seasonal hobby, when winter nights are long, and a congenial and satisfying interest is sought. When spring comes, most stick dressers put away horn and wood to return to with zest in autumn.

The basis of the hobby is an ample selection of shanks. Horn may be scarce, but one-piece and wooden head crooks can still be made. The best time to gather shanks is in autumn and early winter, when the sap is down. The exact period varies from year to year, and certainly between districts; spring and sap-rise reach Somerset and Dorset many weeks before the northern uplands.

Once you have been bitten by the stick dressing bug, any country walk tends to become a search for shanks, the eye seeking out potential straight pieces to add to the shank store. If an exceptional individual stick is found in mid-summer, should it be cut? Many a good stick dresser would say 'yes'. The alternative is to leave it and retrieve it in autumn, but there are two risks to this. The first is that you may not be able to find it, and the second is that someone else will. There is much to be said for cutting a stick when you see it: it prevents those feelings of righteous indignation which arise when a favourite stick has been watched for weeks, growing straight and true, and then is taken by another before its rounded perfection can be put to use.

A stick collecting venture demands proper organisation. Woods or spinneys containing suitable shanks should be sought out, and the owners approached. At the gathering's end, make sure that the plantation is left in tidy and workmanlike condition, with no untidy branches draped around.

TOOLS

The expedition will probably entail walking, possibly over some distance. Tools should, therefore, be kept to the minimum, for not only must they be carried there and back, but the shanks themselves become a considerable burden. A Bushman saw, a hand saw and a bill axe or medium weight axe are needed. Do not forget cords to tie the shanks into bundles. If root sticks are contemplated, a spade should also be carried.

TYPES OF SHANK

The different types of stick or crook must be borne in mind when cutting shanks. For the horn headed

*Block with shanks growing from it. This section of a
branch is left to dry for two years, then sawn so that
the block becomes the shaped head. Roots with
shanks attached are cut and dried similarly.*

stick and crook, the shank must be long and straight. If in doubt about length, measure fourteen hands, one over the other, which gives about four feet eight inches minimum, sufficient for most purposes.

A curve in the shank does not matter as much as a 'dog leg', in which growth has changed course at a knot. There is little point in cutting inferior shanks; unseen troubles can arise in the horn, but the shanks must be above suspicion.

When selecting these straight shanks, bear in mind what is at either end of them, especially the base. They may be growing out from a branch in such a fashion as to have a potential head for a wooden stick, or from roots that would make useful knobs. The other end may have an ideal Y, just right for an easy thumb stick. Thumb sticks are usually plentiful enough, and some experts regard a thumb stick as 'a good shank wasted'; but a wide Y with stout prongs should be carefully considered.

WOOD STICKS

The one-piece stick is fashioned from a straight wand growing out of a branch or root. Hazel and holly are the chief woods for this. The large, mature hazel may have branches spread-eagled at 45 degrees, and some almost horizontal. Try to visualise the size and type of head that may be fashioned from the branch where it gives rise to the upright wand, which will become the shank. Saw off the branch well away from the joint, on the side further from the root. Then saw off the other side, again leaving ample space in case the branch splinters and ruins the junction.

When safely at ground level, the length may be shortened to make carrying easier, but a cardinal rule in stick dressing is that you can take off but seldom put on. To prevent splintering, the woodman's trick is to saw a light groove on the underside of the branch first.

ROOT STICKS

These are more difficult to harvest. An old hazel clump may have a score of potential shanks springing from the bole. Some are cut purely as shanks, while others grow from the root in a way that could provide a natural head, or at least a knob.

Only by digging down can the quantity of root be ascertained. It may be necessary to demolish a fair proportion of the stool to discover the potential, and this is hard and slow work. Even after a number of shanks and their attached roots have been freed from the bole, they will probably not be freed from each other, but will be so intertwined that considerable further sawing and axeing is required.

Such root sticks can be very strong, but they are also heavy in the initial stages, for it is difficult to separate root from lumps of stone and soil. A professional stick maker seldom makes root sticks as they consume far too much time. But for the person seeking the satisfaction of a useful and beautiful aid, they are grand.

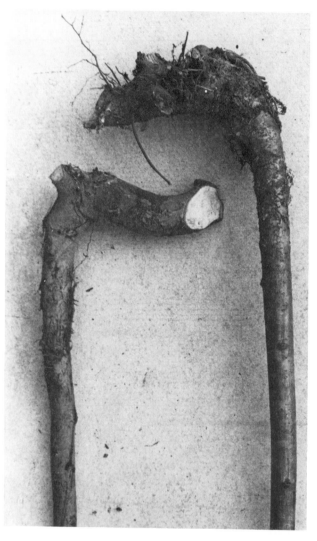

Small roots just below ground level are dug to
provide the basis for a stick head.

LEG CLEEKS

The leg stick or leg cleek is usually made from the branch and wand. A fairly thick branch is needed, depending on the angle of growth, as the cleek is several inches long. It is possible to make a leg cleek by adding horn or hardwood to a straight shank.

STORING

Once the shanks have been brought home, they must be carefully stored. They need at least a year's ripening. Block sticks should stand on the floor, preferably an uninsulated and slightly damp floor, otherwise the blocks may dry out too quickly and split. Obviously, the more the block can be trimmed before storing, the less wood is left to dry out, but do not take risks by over-trimming.

Shanks with no block attached are best stored in bundles of about twelve. Select a straight, solid one for the centre, and build up the bundle around it, tying firmly at several points. Then put on the rafters or otherwise hang up to dry.

Single sticks may be hung by the head, and weighted at the other end, but this is too finicky for most of us. Stick dressing must never become a chore.

Once in store, the shanks tend to be forgotten, so an application of a good insecticide is a worthwhile precaution. Blocks should be examined periodically, and if splits appear, a dressing of linseed oil helps.

Len Parkin with a bundle of shanks ready for drying. At least a year is needed.

Decorative effect of honeysuckle growing round the shank. Shank with pin or dowel (right).

LABELLING

As they go into store, all bundles and blocks should be labelled, giving place and date. It is surprisingly easy to forget in which year a stick was cut. The place name is a reminder of the environment from which it was taken.

SPECIAL TRAINING

The stick dresser usually cuts what shanks he can find, but there is one exception. Honeysuckle climbing round a young tree leaves a spiralling groove very attractive in the finished stick. Honeysuckles may be planted at the base of likely specimens, or trained round a nearby one. The bark of hazel or ash grows under the entwining honeysuckle, forming a pattern that no tool can match.

4 · Types of
Stick and Crook

Sticks and crooks fall into five chief divisions. These are:

One-piece, all wood.
Horn head and wood shank.
Wood head, joined later to the shank.
Thumb stick.
Knob stick.

ONE-PIECE

An interesting type for the beginner is the one-piece stick or crook. The difference between the two is simply the size of the head; even if you have no sheep, you may still prefer a stick for walking fashioned in crook shape and size.

The head is sawn out of the branch or root from which the shank is growing. The size of the block limits the head size; in some cases only a knob is left, and a well-balanced knob stick can be very attractive.

It may be possible to furnish a leg cleek from a branch or root. That is generally a specialist shepherd's tool, and is not usually used as a walking stick. It does, however, have its charms, and anyone

A very fine one-piece wood stick.

making a collection of the different types of sticks and crooks should certainly include one.

The main problem with a one-piece arises if the grain on the head runs parallel to the shank; it is then fairly easily snapped off. But that is not necessarily the end of the stick, for modern glues are so effective that a lasting joint may be re-established. A grain that follows the head round is less liable to snap, and best of all is a tough root that will withstand any amount of knocking. Blackthorn is one example of such a root, and a briar or wild rose root is also strong.

HORN HEAD, WOOD SHANK

In this type of stick, the raw materials are the horn and the shank. They will be married together by a wood dowel or a metal bolt. The other refinements are ferrules at the neck and tip, and pieces of horn to strengthen and decorate the finished article.

The size of horn determines the size of the head, and while it is not too difficult to acquire horn sufficient for a walking stick, something more substantial is needed for a crook.

There is another type intermediate between the horn head and the one-piece wood stick. In this, the horn is used only to make the final curve of the stick, the shank providing the first part. This entails a shank with a half-curve, insufficient to complete the head, and requires less horn. An advantage of this is that ewe horn may be utilised, which is much more readily available than other horns, though varying

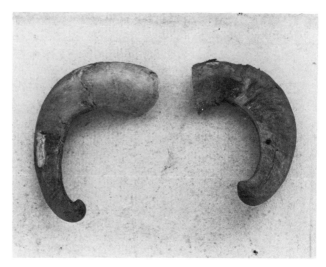

*Smaller horns suitable only for walking sticks
or half-heads.*

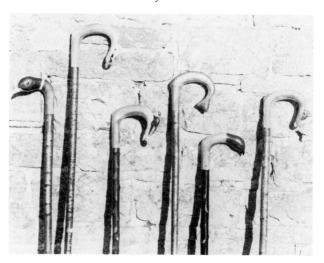

Superb examples of decorated horn heads.

considerably in quality. The half-horn head is brought into play sometimes to save a well-balanced one-piece stick from wastage if its head has broken off. The crown is the usual breaking point, so the remaining curve serves as base for a horn tip.

The plain horn head walking stick is suitable for novices in horn work. A plain horn head can be a thing of great beauty, brought out by final polishing to a high-class finish. Some of the best stick dressers have favoured this type of stick.

The requirements are some eight inches of solid horn if possible, to give sufficient grip for the average hand. Much more horn is needed for the fancy stick, and fourteen inches for a crook.

Never forget the quality of the shank. No matter how much care is lavished on a horn head, it will never make a satisfactory stick if the shank is ill-balanced, bent, too thick or too thin. An adequate store of shanks from which to choose the perfect one for the job is essential.

WOOD HEAD, SEPARATE FROM THE SHANK

The great advantage of this type of stick is that wood suitable for the head is much easier to obtain than is horn. Requirements for the shank are the same as in the first two categories; straight, or at least capable of being straightened, as near cylindrical as possible, and with attractive mottling, in the case of hazel, as an added bonus.

Most hardwoods make suitable heads. Beech, elm, oak and ash are favourites, but very strong heads may be fashioned from imported hardwoods, old pieces of furniture being a fruitful source. Beech is particularly good for carving, so if additions in the form of dog, weasel or rabbit are intended, a piece big enough to allow for them should be selected. Some beech has very attractive black marks, but is liable to faults; nor is it capable of such a fine finish as elm. Old oak stakes that have been in the ground for decades may provide a head. Toughest of all are the burrs on beech and elm trunks, so contact with local sawmills is worth cultivating. Yew is softer than elm, and also lacks its wonderful grainy finish.

All wooden heads must be really seasoned. It is worth mentioning that the types of wood described above are also suitable for carving ornaments as distinct from heads; animals, chains or any other design form a separate hobby for some stick dressers. Unlike a walking stick, the top is done first, and a good tip is to leave projections like the tail in a solid block until near completion. They are easily knocked off during work.

THUMB STICKS

A popular type of thumb stick is one capped with deer horn, so should really come under the section on horn heads. An entirely different type of horn and technique is involved, however; the antler-tip is used without bending. The popularity of venison and deer stalking as a sport, and the spread of deer

[40]

A selection of excellent plain heads, each with a long, straight shank.

Deer horn makes a very effective thumb stick.

farming, have made supplies of deer horn fairly plentiful. It is not cheap, however, and demand exceeds supply. The antler tips should not be allowed to be too sharp, or may be dangerous.

Otherwise, the thumb stick is generally one-piece wood. Any amount of sticks are found with a V at some point, but really suitable ones are rare. The V should ideally be wide enough to take the thumb without carving out a notch, and the twin spurs should be of equal thickness and leave the shank at identical angles. These simple criteria are not always forthcoming. The difficulty with most one-piece thumb sticks is that they tend to taper thickly towards the base. In the case of holly, the excess may be planed or filed away, but that is not always so feasible with other woods.

One use of the thumb stick is as a rest for a telescope or even a rifle. Length should suit the individual; it is frequently more than for a crook or walking stick, as the carrying action is different. Some even prefer a very long shank, and grip it below the head rather than placing the thumb in the V, as is generally the idea.

So easy is the thumb stick to fashion that some stick dressers disregard it. It is likely to remain popular, however, as its ease of carving makes it cheap, and it is a ready seller on the stall.

KNOB STICKS

A ground ash has a ready-made knob, ripe for polishing. Knobs may be fashioned from branch or

*Fox mask carved from a knob on a one-piece stick,
and a deer foot cunningly used.*

root, and although simple and comparatively easy to
carve, can be very effective. Variants such as T-
pieces occur, and do not overlook the possibility of
carving a figure as part of the knob.

[44]

5 · Working the Wood

THE ONE-PIECE

While shanks need twelve months to dry, blocks may well require two years. When that time has elapsed, the first step is to trim the block to the approximate size of the head, always erring on the side of caution when sawing.

Straightening

Having done this rough tidying up, the next step is to straighten the shank. Subject it to moderate heat, protecting the bark by tin foil, or by damping it occasionally with a wet cloth. Do not use too much water, or it will take too long to heat. It is surprising how straightening the shank can alter the angle relative to the head. When the shank is so hot that it cannot readily be held, straighten over the knee while leaning back against a wall or bench, or straighten in the vice. The part most in need of straightening may well be the thickest part quite near the block.

Sawing

Then, look along from the shank and draw two parallel lines to indicate the limit of the sides of the head. Modern marker pens are superior to pencils for this purpose. Saw just outside these lines, leaving slightly greater width at the bottom if desirable. You should now be left with two flat unshaped sides and a straight shank.

It is important to make the saw cuts leaving slightly more than is required for the handle, then the angle may be altered slightly. If you saw to the exact width at the start, there is no room for adjustment later.

Inside Line

Draw the inside line of the head with your marker, allowing three and a half to four inches between the nose and the inside of the heel for a crook, less for a walking stick. The head must be higher at the nose than the heel, or it will never look right. Never draw the top line first; that sequence has been tried and discarded.

With the head secured in a vice, drill or saw round the line; if an electric drill is available, that is probably the quickest way. The drill holes will not meet exactly, so complete with a fret saw or coping saw.

Now rasp out the inside line more accurately, square to the sides. Do not attempt to round off the inside line at this stage. You now have the sawn head with its two flat sides, out of which the under side of the head has been cut away.

Top Line

The marker pen is now used to outline the top of the head. It follows the inner line in the curve desired,

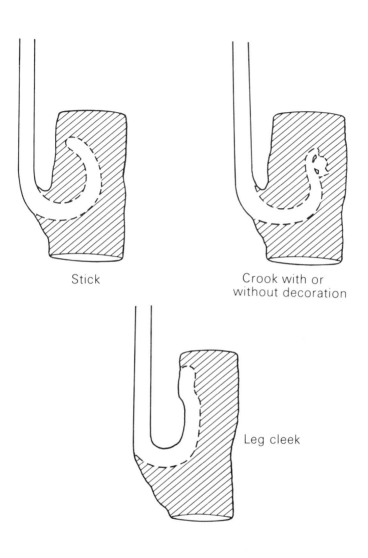

Stick

Crook with or
without decoration

Leg cleek

*Drawing the head of a one-piece; the head you
choose will depend on the quality of the block.*

usually tapering towards the nose. The principle is the same whatever the type of stick: shepherd's crook, walking stick or leg cleek are all fashioned in this sequence.

The top line is more accessible than the inner one, and sawing is easier. The head must be secured in the vice while sawing. Use the best type of saw you possess for a curve or, failing that, saw along the line in three or four straight cuts, and rasp away the intervening wood.

It is not worth being too exact near the nose at this point. A turned-in or turned-up tip to the nose may well be left till later; it is vulnerable, and though the line should show its position, it need not be completed.

Rounding Off

Having achieved the two flat sides of the head, complete with inner and outer shape, rounding off begins. A selection of coarse rasps of varying shapes is a real boon here. The head must be secured in the vice all the while.

As the desired shape takes place, change to a finer rasp or file, for all the file marks must be sand-papered out eventually, and it is better to leave as few as possible for those final stages. The nose should be checked from time to time to ensure it is plumb with the centre of the shank.

Finishing

The head can now be tried in the hand, and any rough parts given further attention. There may be a

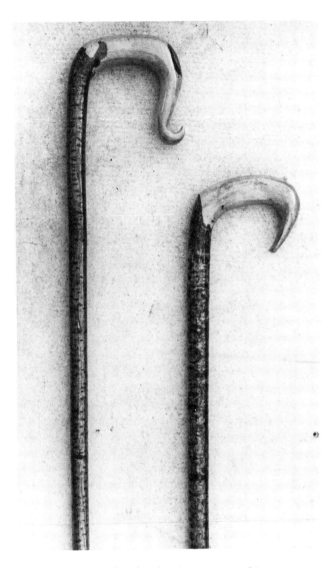

One-piece wood sticks, showing nose turned in or out.

case for leaving a projection where it meets the forefinger or thumb; each case must be decided on its own merits, but always leave the maximum amount of bark. In section, the head can be round or oval, but if the latter, the height must be greater than the width. Use fine files and try to leave a smooth blend of head and shank.

When the files have done their work, rough emery paper can be used for a preliminary smoothing. Then sandpapers of varying degrees of fineness come into play, leaving a smooth finish.

Tipping

As we are dealing with the one-piece wood stick, shanking is not required, and so there is no ferrule. A tip is needed for a high-class job, however, and possibly for showing. It is better to tip all sticks as they are made, because if the job is not done then, the chances are that it will be put off till the end has been roughened by roadwork, and some of the length lost. I have several times had a stick just for 'knocking about', then it has become a favourite, and worthy of a tip to prevent further damage. As that often occurs in summer, out of the normal stick dressing season, the necessary act is further delayed. It is far better to tip a batch of sticks as soon as they are made.

A neat tip to the shank lends a well-finished appearance to the whole stick. If badly done, tipping can spoil the entire effect, so care is needed. Tips can be made from any hard material. Of the horns, deer is hardest and best, while brass, copper or aluminium tubes may also be used.

The operation is straightforward. But first, make quite sure that the shank length is correct, otherwise the tip is wasted. That is one drawback to tipping sticks for sale; the length that suits one customer may not suit another. Measure the length of the tip along the shank and mark it. Then encircle the shank with a mark at that point and saw or cut round shallowly with a fine saw or sharp knife.

The tip has usually been drilled out, often at half an inch. The end of the shank is reduced to this measurement, initially by a sharp knife to remove the bark and then by a rasp. Sandpapering leaves a clean and precise finish. Glue is used to fix a horn tip in position. Some metal tips are punched to keep them in place, but it must be neatly done.

Rubber tips are handy where quiet is essential, and to give a grip on slippery surfaces. Thus they are used in such diverse situations as deer stalking, to avoid metal tips striking rock and warning the quarry, and by the elderly or infirm who are assisted by a secure hold. A neat, stout, well-shod walking stick can be of immense help where walking is difficult.

The Shank

The shank of the one-piece stick was straightened early. Its knots must now be trimmed as neatly as possible, or rather to give maximum effect. On blackthorn a definite projection from each knot may be favoured, while on holly the knots can be rounded to give a ripple. Hazel knots should be trimmed to give a pair of facing half moons; the new white is retained if trimmed just before varnishing.

Care must be taken in sandpapering the shank. Too rough a paper ruins the dappled beauty of hazel, whose bark varies in strength and colour according to a number of factors, including age and place of growing.

Varnishing

A number of suitable varnishes are on the market, but clear polyurethane is the most popular. If others prefer a different varnish, all well and good; the principles of application are much the same.

Dust the shank and head to remove any loose sawdust particles, then apply the varnish with a small paint brush. Several light dressings are far better than one or two thick ones, and twenty-four hours or more for drying must be allowed between each. It will be found that the sandpapered head absorbs more than the bark of the shank, and may need extra coats.

For show sticks, varnish may be applied, allowed to dry, and then lightly rubbed down before a further thin application is given. That is one difference between the exhibition specimen and the run-of-the-mill stick. In some cases a sealer is needed, but in any event great care must be taken to ensure an even finish, as one part of the shank often takes in more varnish than another.

If you are making several sticks, it is often better to have a 'varnishing session' in the toolshop or other convenient building, rather than risk drips in the house.

TWO-PIECE WOOD STICKS

The head and shank are separate pieces of wood in this type. Shanks have already been discussed; the head is cut from well-seasoned hardwood.

Burrs should be stored for at least two, preferably three years. To store, the burr from beech or elm should be cut into slices, rather thicker than the ultimate need. Then, set these slices in an airy situation, but under cover from rain and out of direct sunlight. Sticks are laid on each slice to keep it separate from those above and below, allowing air to circulate. Kiln drying is a means of speeding up the process.

Shaping

After this period, the first stage in carving is to draw the crook or walking stick head in outline on the flat surface. Try to select a solid part for the head itself; burrs often have open bits interspersed with denser wood, and it is better if these open parts coincide with areas to be discarded.

If you already have a favourite head, trace round that, otherwise draw the required design in pencil and, when satisfied, etch in with marker pen. The under line is drawn first and the top line made to follow it.

Now cut out along the bottom line. A series of holes from an electric drill provides the fastest method, or a hand drill or coping saw may be used.

[53]

Len Parkin near his horn shop in the Borders,
holding a slice of burr for making heads.

Head sketched onto wood block before shaping.

Then follow with the saw around the top, remembering always that wood can be removed, but seldom added.

Shanking

At this stage all the cuts are vertical, at right angles to the flat surface. The head has taken rough shape but has not been rounded off. A drill hole of $\frac{1}{2}$ to $\frac{5}{8}$ inch is made into the heel, and the pin or dowel fashioned on the shank.

By shanking at this early stage, the head may be shaped to match the shank. If the whole head is shaped first, you may find that the shank you have selected is too thick for the head, and the combination will never balance properly.

Next take off the head, and shape it in the vice by rounding off the sharp angles. Rasps or Surform files are the most suitable tools, and shank and head can be refitted from time to time to check as the work progresses. Leave the head loose on the shank during these trials. It should not be glued in place until ready for the final polishing. During the fitting, decide which way the shank will be fixed by revolving the head around it. When the best position becomes evident, mark the shank at the front of the toe by slicing off a small piece, or using a marker stick.

General preparation of the shank has already been described. In a two-piece, the head of the shank is inserted into the horn or wood head by means of a pin or dowel. To make this, measure some two inches from the end of the shank, and mark round it with a light saw groove. The length of the pin depends on the length of the hole bored into the head, and this varies.

When the groove has formed a complete circle, the saw cut may be deepened, or the surplus wood removed with a sharp penknife. Work round and round so that the pin is central and exactly in line with the shank. If a mistake is made, the work must start again two inches lower, so do not be in too big a hurry to shorten the shank exactly to its required length.

A smaller peg suffices for a walking stick, compared with a crook. The skilled shepherd can catch a hill ewe rushing past at top speed, and all that sheep's weight and energy is brought to a sudden halt by the head of the crook, so the pin must be strong. The pin may be strengthened by a steel rod. In such cases, the rod is inserted before the pin is shaped. Alternatively, a metal peg may be used, in

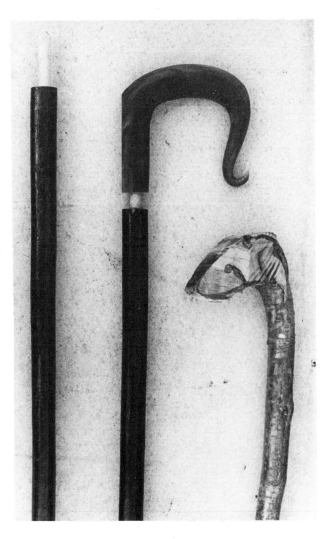

Shank showing pin ready for inserting in the head,
loosely at first (centre). *A one-piece carved*
head ready for completion (right).

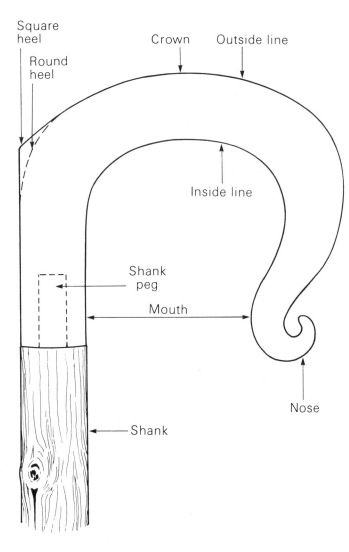

Crook showing shank peg; the peg must be central and exactly in line with the shank.

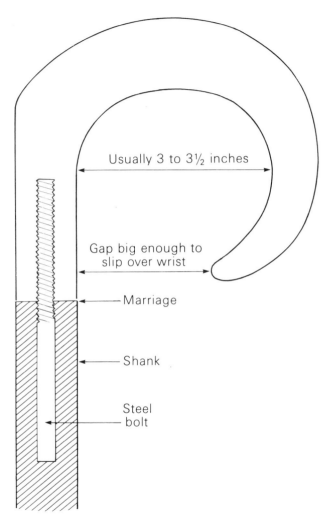

Usually 3 to 3½ inches

Gap big enough to
slip over wrist

— Marriage

— Shank

Steel
— bolt

Plain stick with threaded steel bolt; when a bolt is
used both head and shank are drilled to receive it.

which case both head and shank are bored to receive it.

It cannot be overemphasised that if the shank proves unsuited to the head in size and balance, it must be substituted by another. A cylindrical shank is far better than one with too much taper, and an idea of the final balance may be gained by early shanking, before the final shaping of the head has taken place.

The head must be higher at the nose than at the heel. That applies to both crooks and walking sticks, for a head with a drooping nose will never look right. The relative positions are best assessed when the head is on the shank.

Finishing

Having determined that all is roughly correct, final smoothing and polishing may begin. The inside of the head should be rounded off first, testing for grip with the hand from time to time. A cylindrical or rounded rasp is best for this. Then the top is similarly shaped, and it is often possible to use a flat rasp here.

Head and shank may be glued together when the final rasping has been achieved, but before polishing. Sandpaper the rasp marks until the surface is absolutely smooth, starting with emery paper or strong sandpaper, and using gradually finer grades.

HORN HEAD, WOOD SHANK

The same principles as above apply when making a horn headed crook or stick. The difference is mainly in the size of horn available.

Age

A horn that has matured for at least two years after leaving the sheep is preferable. Unmatured horn never works to the same standard of finish, and is more liable to twist.

Trimming

Set the horn in a vice and saw off the thick end more or less square, but taking no more off than necessary. Trim the roughest excrescences, and file away the inner rim which often appears as an almost sharp projection. Judicious trimming at this stage leaves less mass to heat.

Heating

Horn becomes workable and pliable only when hot. There are various forms of suitable heat, the simplest for a heavy old horn being to boil it for a couple of hours.

Another method is the bottled gas burner, which achieves the same result. It is essential to hold the horn in the hand, moving it about in the flame held in the other hand. To leave either horn or burner in a fixed position is to invite scorching. Brush on a thin coat of machine oil as protection.

A dish of methylated spirits is used by some of the

best stick dressers. It gives a safe heat, and the horn is worked along it in sections. When the nose is reached, a pair of pliers may be necessary to apply the final stages of heating.

A peat fire is another possibility, and the first sticks were all made on peat fires in shepherds' cottages. The drawback is that it is more difficult to apply the heat exactly where needed.

Squeezing

When horn is thoroughly heated it becomes quite workable, but only trial and error can indicate when the necessary state has been reached. The first stage is to flatten the horn. A mature ram's horn may have two or three curls, and all must be brought into the same plane. To do this, a strong vice with flat plates is needed. Open the vice to the anticipated necessary width; there is no point in losing heat while screwing out the vice. Insert the horn, starting at the nose (the part furthest from the head), and tighten the vice, a section at a time if necessary. The only exception to this procedure is if a walking stick with an angled curl is being made.

The Heel

After squeezing into one plane, the next step is to squeeze up the heel. It may be hollow, the degree of solidity being an important factor. Very shelly horns are of little use, and the thin part must be sawn away until something better is arrived at.

To squeeze the heel, bushes or half-round pipe sections are needed. They may be of metal or wood.

It is relatively simple to construct oak bushes that function admirably. The heel should be squeezed from different angles until it becomes virtually solid. Then the rest of the horn is similarly squeezed, finishing with a round rather than the original triangular section. Squeezing continues right to the tip of the horn, aiming for maximum thickness all the time.

Shaping

Reheating will now be necessary, after which the inside radius of the horn should be placed against a hardwood block of the desired shape and squeezed up in the vice, until the horn follows exactly the outer shape of the block.

The nose may point inwards, following the same curve as the crown and its continuation, or it may be twisted outwards, the site of possible decoration. For a crook, the outward nose is essential, to guide the crook onto the sheep's neck. Grips or a metal cylinder are used to impart this twist, and to assist shaping generally.

Shanking

The head is fixed in a vice, and rasped and filed into rough shape. It must fit snugly in the hand; square edges must be removed, leaving a slightly oval section. Before final rasping and polishing, shanking must be done. The heel is sawn either square, or at the angle desired where it meets the shank. An angled 'marriage' can be very effective, but a square one is safer for beginners.

*Opposite sides of the same ram's horn after the
initial clamping in a vice. Some of the roughness
may be filed away before heating.*

*A section of ram's horn, showing the hollow part
that must be squeezed solid after heating.*

*A flattened horn, and the shaped head
that it may become.*

[65]

*Alternative ways of shaping the horn; the nose is
bent either in or out.*

A ½ or ⅝ inch hole is then drilled into the horn
head, as described for the wood head, and the shank
is given a dowel or pin to fit the drilled hole. Decide
on a suitable shank, but do not glue the two
together yet. Binding with insulation tape just
below the 'marriage' protects the shank when the
horn is being worked.

After heating, it is better to allow the horn to cool

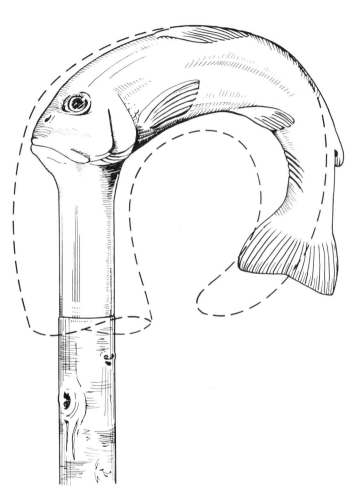

*Shaping a fish from rough horn; the inside radius of the
horn should be squeezed against a hardwood block
of the desired shape.*

in its own time. The cooling process can be speeded by using a wet cloth, but horn tends to revert to its original shape, and that is less likely if allowed to cool slowly.

Once it is thoroughly cool, further straightening may be decided on. The nose must be absolutely in line with the heel. If it is a little to one side, re-heat and straighten.

Horn has a whiter, softer interior, and it is part of the stick dresser's art to prevent that part from surfacing. Any visible white should ideally be covered by hard horn in the squeezing process.

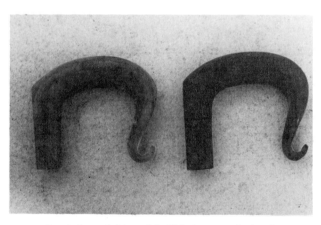

Ram's horn (left) *and buffalo horn ready for the final shanking and finishing.*

THUMB STICKS

Among the simplest sticks to fashion are thumb sticks, but there is a wide range between a really smart, nicely balanced thumb stick and a nondescript object. Thumb sticks are normally one-piece, except where deer horn is used.

The type of wood to use has already been discussed. The two prongs should come out at a fairly wide angle and should really match each other, though this is not essential except in a show stick. The shank should not have too much taper; if, as so often happens, the prongs emerge at a slender point, the shank is bottom-heavy.

The length of the shank varies with the individual, but it is always longer than for the conventional walking stick; about forty-eight to fifty inches to the base of the Y is the average. The shank must be straightened before shaping. To do this, cut off the prongs squarely, about three or four inches from their base, although their length is largely a matter of taste. Make them the same length, and then round the tops with a knife, rasp or Surform. A rounded crown is effective and safe. It may be necessary to cut away slightly at the base of the Y to give thumb room, particularly with a narrow angle. The shank must then be dressed and possibly tipped as described for the one-piece stick.

Deer horn thumb sticks are popular. The antler points readily lend themselves to this form of stick. Match shank to horn as a first step, then shape the shank head to fit into the hollow of the horn. It may

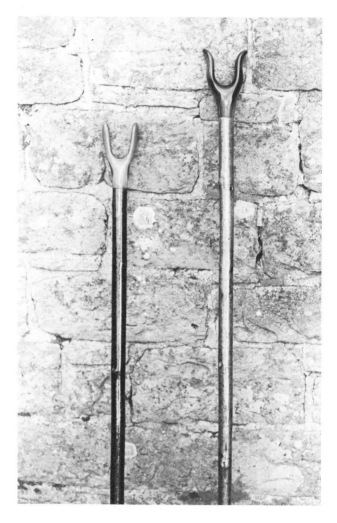

Unusual thumb sticks from cow and buffalo horn.

be necessary to remove any very sharp points on the horn. It is easier to choose a suitable shank for this type of thumb stick, which makes good use of a longer than average quality shank.

Rough-cut thumb sticks (left), *before shaping and varnishing* (right).

KNOB STICKS

Like the thumb stick, the knob stick can be easily and quickly made, although again, the difference between a run-of-the-mill stick and a highly polished, well-finished one is considerable. This stick is ideal for certain types of infirmity, as it allows the full weight of arm and shoulder to be

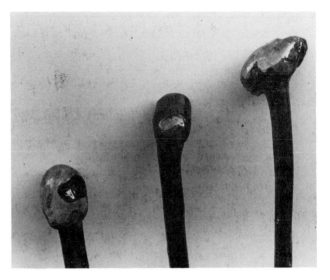

Knobs are the simplest, yet very effective, means of using small pieces of branch or root.

taken directly. To that end, length is important, varying with the individual; so is strength of shank – a strong and true shank is needed if an aid to lameness is sought. If an ideal one is found for this purpose, furnish it with a tip immediately, or wear and tear will soon reduce the length to below that which is most comfortable.

It is often feasible to fashion a knob stick from a branch or root attached to the shank that is insufficient to make either a one-piece walking stick head or crook. Saw down the knob to the desired maximum size before dressing, and then straighten

[72]

the shank. In a stick of this kind, the part of the shank nearest the knob may well be so thick as to make straightening difficult, in which case take that part as the line and straighten the rest of the shank in line with it. Balance is important, and a well-made knob stick sits comfortably in the hand.

After the initial sawing, rasp the knob until the desired roundness is achieved. Follow this with emery paper and sandpaper, and smooth the shank. The exposed wood of the knob will require more coats of varnish than the barked shank, possibly even a sealer.

LEG CLEEK

Of all sticks, the leg cleek is least used for general purposes, but is invaluable to the shepherd. It is used to take the sheep on the hind leg, just above the hock, and withdraw it backwards from the flock. In this respect, it is far better than a neck crook when working in a densely packed flock. Sheer weight of numbers makes insertion of the neck crook difficult, while the same massed weight of sheep makes drawing her out a tiresome occupation. There can be danger in ill-use of the cleek, as if twisted it can injure the sheep's leg, but that would only happen through carelessness.

Horn or wood may be used for the cleek head. Its dimensions are very important; the mouth should be the width of an old halfpenny, widening out into a space the maximum width of an old penny. Length is in proportion, usually about four inches, and the

Leg cleek, a highly practical shepherd's tool for catching a sheep by the hind leg, just above the hock, and drawing her out backwards from the flock with minimum fuss.

nose should sweep away from the straight side to guide in the leg.

The shank should be comparatively short, as the shepherd is using the cleek with his arm fully extended and a very long shank would be a disadvantage. It should also be cylindrical. That is important because during action the shepherd is holding the foot of the crook and not the head. Otherwise, principles of making are the same as for a horn head, wood head or one-piece.

Being unusual, leg cleeks may become sought after. At one dog show an American visitor was so taken with the one I was carrying that he offered a handsome price for it. Here is one advantage of the hobby of stick dressing: the finished product may often be sold without any positive sales campaign. But a particular favourite will never be sold.

6 · Showing

EVENTS

The Royal Highland Show stages nine classes for sticks and crooks, the Great Yorkshire Show, thirteen. Many other agricultural shows have a number of classes, and in the stick dressing areas of Northumberland and the Borders they form a major part of the exhibition. There is a fascination about sticks that draws visitors from all walks of life, and the British Field Sports Society and other rural organisations frequently display sticks as an adjunct to their main business, chiefly to attract interest.

The novice stick dresser probably begins with no competitive ambitions; to carve and own a neat, well-balanced stick from natural materials is satisfaction enough. But it is surprising how soon the beginner will note the well-filled racks at the local show, and decide that his is as good as some of those displayed.

The best of one's own work may be entered, initially more to support the event than with any real hope of winning. Competition is so keen that to enter a show class calls for a positive decision, and also for horn and shank of the necessary quality.

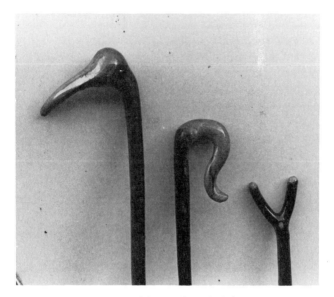

Curlew head carved from a branch (left), *one-piece leg cleek* (centre) *and simple thumb stick.*

CLASSIFICATION

It is vital to read and understand the schedules properly. Many a good stick is thrown out by the judge simply because it is in the wrong category, rather than through any inherent fault. If in doubt, consult the secretary, for there is sometimes a thin distinction between paint or varnish being allowed in a particular class, and rules are often strict. The Royal Highland and Agricultural Society of Scotland dates back to 1784, and has very specific rules about clear varnish, paint and artificial colouring, and the use of plastic bands. It also requires that horn, where used, is from British breeds of sheep or goats, or from native cattle horns, red deer or roe deer antlers.

PRIZES

The honour of a red ticket rather than the value of prize money is the incentive where sticks are concerned. Border Union prizes in 1984 were £2, £1 and 50p. Great Yorkshire prizes in that year were £4, £3 and £2 with a perpetual rose bowl for the champion on a points basis. There is also the Lammermuir perpetual cup for the novice (an exhibitor who has not won a first prize previous to the current year) for the best walking stick with a plain handle of horn or hazel.

STANDARDS

Show classes in the main stick dressing areas are now of a very high standard. Yet in recent years there have been criticisms that a proportion of the entries have been under-finished. This should encourage the novice; finish is largely a matter of time and application, of a willingness to persevere with varnish time after time, rubbing down again after each coat has dried.

The chief difference between the exhibition stick and the one for everyday use lies in this vital matter

The pheasant's head is an intricate but favourite model.

of finish. Naturally, an ill-balanced crook with the smartest head stands no chance, but a really smooth finish is essential.

JUDGES

Show committees have a perennial problem in finding suitable judges for their numerous events. If the judge is a stick dresser of some repute, all is reasonably well. The trouble arises when a judge has carried a stick for most of his life, but has never made one. The good judge will act not just on appearances, but will handle the sticks before selecting his winner. Like a well-balanced gun or cricket bat, the master stick feels as though it is swinging up of its own accord when held by the rigid arm.

It is a poor principle to avoid a particular show on account of the judge, but if the adjudicator has known likes and dislikes, these must be taken into account. Some judges, especially north of the Border, might prefer the thistle above all other decorations, and many others have their own particular favourite decorations. Intricate ornamentation and the plain horn head are two extremes unlikely to be favoured by the same person, although of course these types will be in different classes.

DISPLAY

Standards of display have improved in recent years and there was certainly room for improvement. It is quite unfair to push sticks into a rough rack where all and sundry can handle them, and at the show's end leave them in a corner till the owners arrive. The sticks are best arranged in tidy racks with footholes, roped off just out of reach of spectators. A bench or table should be provided, on which the judge can lay his final selections.

On arrival at the show, the steward should number but not name each stick, and the judge should not be told the owners' identities, which means that he must not see a catalogue beforehand. The steward is there to help the judge, and pass him any sticks he asks for, not to offer his own opinions on the sticks.

A good judge will pace up and down with the sticks he fancies, and try them for balance by swinging with the extended arm from both the head and the tip. He is aware that someone will be disappointed after scores of hours spent painstakingly carving and polishing. But in the end, it is a question of individual choice, and the judge can only select the one that he would most like to take home.

Curled ram's horn head (left) *with other simple yet pleasing carvings from root or branch.*

SHOW POINTS

Fancy decorated and carved sticks may look worlds apart from a plain walking stick, but the basic points are the same and must be considered on the show bench.

Balance

The importance of this has already been mentioned; a stick that feels 'numb' when picked up, does not compare with one that swings almost like a live thing. Even after the stick has been completed, balance can be altered if the shank is at fault, by dressing down the part spoiling the effect. That entails revarnishing, and so is seldom worthwhile, but it can be done.

The nose of the stick or crook must be in dead centre. Viewed from the front, it must be right in line with the centre of the shank, not edging to one side. Obviously, that does not apply to a curled head where the horn sweeps around itself on one side.

Junctions must be exact. The 'marriage' of the head and shank may be at right angles or at a slight angle. In either case, there must be no untidy line and, though the stick is probably tapering at that point, the line of head and shank must continue smoothly, with no bulges or depressions.

Ferrules

If a ferrule is used, its diameter may be slightly more than the head and shank it unites, but it must not spoil the line. Countersunk ferrules continue the

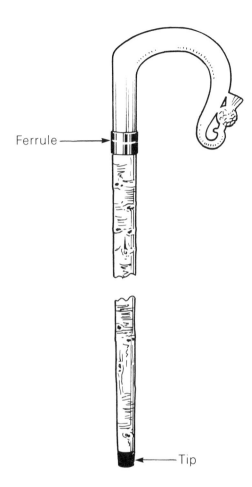

Ferrule

Tip

*A ferrule may be proud or flush, but must not spoil
the line of the stick; a tip must fit exactly.*

line exactly, but for show purposes are not classed
above the other type. The ferrule itself must be a
thing of beauty, but it can also be used to hide a flaw
in the joint, and so is regarded by some as suspect.

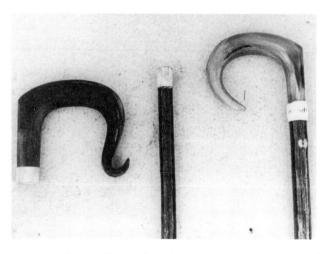

Ferrules: on the tip of the shank for protection (left)
and at the 'marriage' of shank and head.

Ferrules for strength, durability and decoration.

Tips

If a tip is used, it must fit precisely. It is another kind of ferrule, usually, though not always, with a solid end. Brass, copper, horn or other serviceable materials can be used. An untipped stick is an unfinished stick, the tip's main purpose being to prevent the wooden shank being worn away on roads or stony ground. It is not essential in a show class, but where it is used, it must be an enhancement of the whole.

Shanks

An attractive shank is vital. The most ornately carved head will not win prizes if crudely attached to a shank not of the highest order. Straightness is essential, while in the case of hazel a pleasing, dappled bark helps the appearance of the shank. The shank must be suitable for the head; a tiny horn head makes an acceptable child's or lady's walking stick, but a shank of similar fineness must be used. Equally, a large head must have a shank matched in weight and thickness.

Heads

The viewing public sees the head first. Show sticks come only from near-perfect heads, and those that disclose some fault in the later stages of finishing are not show material. Finishing entails hours of varnishing, rubbing down and polishing; this degree of finish is essential when competing in the top bracket.

Very neat grouse adorning the nose, making a plain stick quite outstanding.

Ornaments

Figures on the head should be carved from the whole, not stuck on afterwards. Sometimes it is difficult to differentiate, but the dedicated stick dresser does not lower his standards by adding a stoat, weasel or sheep from a separate block. Detail must be accurate, and the scales on a fish take much

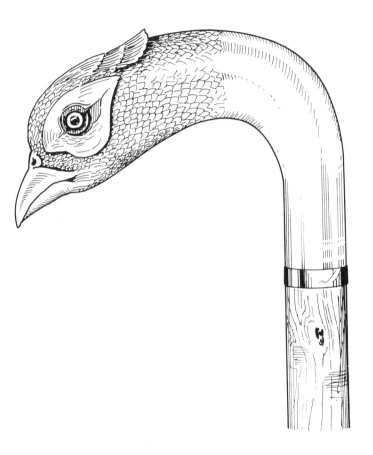

*A pheasant's head worked from horn, engraved and
coloured. Detail must be accurate.*

skill to copy exactly. Similarly with dogs; the Border Collie is naturally favoured on shepherds' crooks, but do not forget that every Border Collie has a white tip to its tail! Judges are invariably country people even if not always accomplished stick dressers themselves, and they will seek authenticity in any models carved, as well as assessing the neatness of the handiwork.

Appendix

SELECTED SHOW CLASSES

Open competitions for 'Shepherds' Crooks Etc' at the Border Union Show, Kelso, Roxburghshire, in late July are:

Walking Stick, plain wood, one-piece.
Walking Stick, plain horn head.
Walking Stick, fancy wood.
Walking Stick, fancy horn head.
Neck Crook, plain wood, one-piece.
Neck Crook, plain horn head.
Neck Crook, fancy wood.
Neck Crook, fancy horn head.
Leg Cleek, plain wood, one-piece.
Leg Cleek, plain horn head.
Novice Crook or Stick.
Sportsman's Class.
Thumb Stick, natural.
Thumb Stick, two-piece.

The classes of The Royal Highland and Agricultural Society of Scotland are:

Crook, horn head with suitable ornamentation.

Crook, in one piece, with suitable ornamentation.
Crook, with plain horn head.
Crook, in one piece, with plain head.
Leg Cleek, with plain horn head.
Leg Cleek, in one piece, with plain head.
Walking Stick, with horn head.
Walking Stick, with or without horn head, with fancy ornamentation.
Walking Stick, in one piece.

The Great Yorkshire Show at Harrogate in the second week of July has stick classes in the Forestry Section. In 1984 they comprised:

Walking Stick, in one piece, hand-made (not painted or artificially coloured) – twelve entries.
Walking Stick, horn head, hand-made (not painted or artificially coloured) – fourteen entries.
Leg Stick or Crook in one piece, hand-made (not painted or artificially coloured) –eleven entries.
Leg Stick or Crook, horn head, hand-made, (not painted or artificially coloured) –ten entries.
Thumb Stick, in one or two pieces, in wood or horn, hand-made (not painted or artificially coloured) – seventeen entries.
Shepherd's Crook, in one piece, hand-made (not painted or artificially coloured) –eleven entries.
Shepherd's Crook, horn head, hand-made (not painted or artificially coloured) –twelve entries.
Pair of Crooks, one horn and one wood, for the championship of Yorkshire (not painted or

artificially coloured) – ten entries.

Walking Stick, in one piece, made by competitors living in England, north of the Trent –twelve entries.

Thumb Stick, in one piece, made by competitors living in England, north of the Trent –thirteen entries.

Walking Stick, of wood and/or horn, carved and decorated, which may be painted or coloured – eleven entries.

Walking Stick, of wood and/or horn, carved and decorated, which may be painted or coloured, made by competitors living in England, north of the Trent –ten entries.

Walking Stick, horn or wood (not painted or artificially coloured) hand-made by a novice who has not won a first prize previous to the current year –eight entries.

Stick making demonstrations are given daily at this and several other major shows where stick classes are staged. The craftsmen answer individual questions and are generally extremely helpful.

Index

Italic numerals denote the page numbers of illustrations